Leroy Milton Yale

## The Academy as a Teacher

An Anniversary Discourse Delivered before the New York Academy of

Medicine, December 11, 1879

Leroy Milton Yale

**The Academy as a Teacher**
*An Anniversary Discourse Delivered before the New York Academy of Medicine,*
*December 11, 1879*

ISBN/EAN: 9783337816391

Printed in Europe, USA, Canada, Australia, Japan

Cover: Foto ©Thomas Meinert / pixelio.de

More available books at **www.hansebooks.com**

# NEW YORK ACADEMY OF MEDICINE.

## 1879.

# ANNIVERSARY DISCOURSE.

BY

# LEROY M. YALE, M.D.

# New York Academy of Medicine,

INSTITUTED, 1847.     INCORPORATED, 1851.

*12 West Thirty-first Street.*

Regular Meetings, First and Third Thursday Evenings in the Month.

~~~~~~~~~~~~~~~~

## OFFICERS FOR 1879.

# COMMITTEES FOR 1879.

### Committee on Admissions.

MARK BLUMENTHAL, M.D., *Chairman*,    JOSEPH E. JANVRIN, M.D.,
T. MATLACK CHEESMAN, M.D.,    ELLSWORTH ELIOT, M.D.,
EDWARD H. JANES, M.D.

### Committee on Medical Ethics.

T. MATLACK CHEESMAN, M.D., *Chairman*,    JOHN C. PETERS, M.D.,
JAMES L. BANKS, M.D.,    *OLIVER WHITE, M.D.,
F. V. WHITE, M.D., *Secretary*.

### Committee on Medical Education.

FRANK H. HAMILTON, M.D., LL.D., *Ch'man*,    FREDERICK A. BURRALL, M.D.,
CHARLES C. LEE, M.D.,    ALFRED C. POST, M.D., LL.D.,
CHARLES W. PACKARD, M.D., *Secretary*.

### Committee on Library.

E. DARWIN HUDSON, JR., M.D., *Chairman*,    LAURENCE JOHNSON, M.D.
GEORGE BAYLES, M.D.,    JOSEPH WIENER, M.D.,
JOHN H. HINTON, M.D., *Secretary*.

### Committee on Ways and Means.

JAMES ANDERSON, M.D.,    WILLARD PARKER, M.D.,
SAMUEL T. HUBBARD, M.D.,    JARED LINSLY, M.D.,
JOHN G. ADAMS, M.D.,    STEPHEN SMITH, M.D.,
SAMUEL S. PURPLE, M.D.,    GOUVERNEUR M. SMITH, M.D.

### Committee on Building.

SAMUEL S. PURPLE, M.D.,    GOUVERNEUR M. SMITH, M.D.

~~~~~~~~~~~~~~~~

# SECTIONS.

### Section on Surgery.

Regular Meeting, Second Tuesday Evening in the Month.
STEPHEN SMITH, M.D., *Chairman*,    A. B. DE LUNA, M.D., *Secretary*.

### Section on Theory and Practice of Medicine.

Regular Meeting, Third Tuesday Evening in the Month.
EDWIN F. WARD, M.D., *Chairman*,    W. H. KATZENBACH, M.D., *Sec'y*.

### Section on Obstetrics and Diseases of Women and Children.

Regular Meeting, Fourth Thursday Evening in the Month.
SALVATORE CARO, M.D., *Chairman*,    HENRY E. CRAMPTON, M.D., *Secretary*.

---

* Deceased.

# PUBLICATIONS OF THE ACADEMY.

*The following Publications of the NEW YORK ACADEMY OF MEDICINE can be obtained of the Librarian, at the prices affixed ; or the same may be had in exchange for medical works, etc., not already in the Library.*

## TRANSACTIONS.

First Series. Vol. I. Pages 461. ⎫
          Vol. II.    "   454. ⎬ Each........................$2.50
          Vol. III.   "   476. ⎭

Second Series. Vol. I. Pages 429. ⎫ Each.....................$4.00
           Vol. II.   "   502. ⎭

## BULLETIN.

Vol. I. Pages 588. ⎫
Vol. II.   "   562. ⎬
Vol. III.   "   470. ⎬ Each.........................................$2.00
Vol. IV.   "   264. ⎭

☞ Single Parts of the above will be sold separately (when complete sets are not broken) at the rate of TEN cents for every *sixteen* pages.

## ADDRESSES AND MEMOIRS.

Dr. John W. Francis' Anniversary Discourse....................1847. $0 25
Dr. John W. Francis' Inaugural Address.......................1848.    10
Dr. James R. Manley's Anniversary Discourse..................1848.    25
Dr. Valentine Mott's Inaugural Address ......................1849.    10
Dr. Alfred C. Post's Anniversary Oration....................1849.    25
Dr. Isaac Wood's Inaugural Address..........................1850.    10
Dr. Joseph M. Smith's Anniversary Discourse................. 1850.    25
Dr. Thomas Cock's Inaugural Address........................1852.    10
Dr. F. Campbell Stewart's Anniversary Discourse.... .........1852.    25
Dr. E. Delafield's Biographical Sketch of J. Kearny Rodgers, M.D.1852.    25
Dr. John H. Griscom's Anniversary Discourse .................1854.    25
Dr. John Watson's Anniversary Discourse, "The Medical Profes-
  sion in Ancient Times"...................................1855.  1 00
Dr. J. M. Sims' Anniversary Discourse,"Silver Sutures in Surgery" 1857.    50
Dr. J. P. Batchelder's Inaugural Address....................1858.    10
Dr. E. R. Peaslee's Anniversary Discourse, " The Progress and
  the Spirit of Medical Science "...........................1858.    50
Dr. Wm. C. Roberts' Anniversary Discourse...................1859.    25
Dr. John Watson's Anniversary Discourse,"The True Physician ".1860.    25
Dr. James Anderson's Inaugural Address......................1861.    10
Dr. V. Mott's Eulogy on Dr. J. W. Francis...................1861.    25
Dr. S. Conant Foster's Anniversary Address..................1862.    25
Dr. John W. Draper's Anniversary Discourse..................1863.    25
Dr. A. C. Post's Eulogy on Dr. Valentine Mott.  Steel Portrait..1865.    50
Portrait of Dr. V. Mott. on India Paper. Small 4to, 50c.; large 4to.  1 00
Dr. James Anderson's Valedictory Address...................1867.    20
Dr. Gouverneur M. Smith's Anniversary Discourse. ...........1873.    25
Dr. John C. Dalton's Anniversary Discourse..................1873.    25
Dr. D. B. St. John Roosa's Anniversary Discourse........ ....1874.    15
Dr. Austin Flint's Valedictory and Dr. Purple's Inaugural........1875.    15
Dr. E. Darwin Hudson, Jr.'s, Anniversary Discourse...........1875.    15
Dr. Wm. T. White's Anniversary Discourse.....................1876.    20
Dr.S.S. Purple's Inaugural Address on " Medical Libraries in N.Y.".1877.    20
Dr. T. Gaillard Thomas' Anniversary Discourse...............1877.    20
Dr. William H. Thomson's Anniversary Discourse..............1878.    20
Dr. Purple's Valedictory, and Dr. Barker's Inaugural...........1879.    20
Dr. Leroy M. Yale's Anniversary Discourse...................1879.    20

# THE ACADEMY AS A TEACHER.

## AN
# ANNIVERSARY DISCOURSE

### DELIVERED BEFORE THE NEW YORK ACADEMY OF MEDICINE, DECEMBER 11, 1879.

## LEROY M. YALE, M.D.,

LECTURER ADJUNCT UPON ORTHOPEDIC SURGERY IN BELLEVUE HOSPITAL MEDICAL COLLEGE; SURGEON TO BELLEVUE HOSPITAL, NEW YORK.

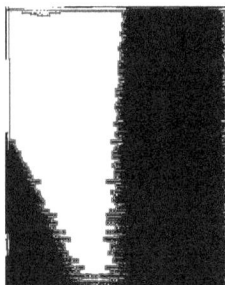

## NEW YORK:
## PRINTED FOR THE ACADEMY,
### 12 WEST THIRTY-FIRST STREET.
### 1879.

# ANNIVERSARY ADDRESS.

*MR. PRESIDENT AND FELLOWS OF THE ACADEMY:*

SYDNEY SMITH is said to have remarked of the late Earl Russell, " Lord John is neither a surgeon nor a sailor, but such is his self-confidence that at two hours' notice he would cut for stone or take command of the Channel fleet." It has occurred to me that in accepting at short notice the office of orator for this evening, I have manifested a degree of assurance li.tle short of that attributed to the English statesman. Yet, when I say that I have always esteemed the position a peculiarly honorable one, and that it was tendered to me by one of your former Presidents with his matchless persuasiveness of manner, you will, I am sure, cease to wonder that I for the moment forgot my unfitness for the task, and rashly accepted it ; and you will, I hope, leniently pardon the absence from my address of that learning and eloquence to which you have become accustomed on occasions like this.

If it were in my power ever to make an interesting address, I should particularly desire to make it now. For never has the Academy been so prosperous, never has its position been so dignified, never have its prospects of a career of long-continued activity and usefulness been so bright as now. And the fitness of things would seem to demand that the address of to-night should in some degree accord with these cheering circumstances.

Naturally, my own memory of the Academy does not run back to the time of which the founders tell us, when the Fel-

ject of my remarks to-night. But let me hasten to reassure you
by saying that I do not propose to discuss how medical schools
shall educate, but how we here may educate; and less how we
shall teach the undergraduate than how we shall teach our-
selves. The recent very general discussion of the preparation
of students for our profession has been directed, I think, too
much toward how we are to control their education, and too
little to how we are to help it. There is little disagreement as
to the shortcomings of American medical education, and of
the disadvantages of the plan of its control; but when the ques-
tion is fairly put, " how will you improve it, or where else
would you prefer to place its government?" the answer is
neither prompt nor definite. While we await opportunities, let
us see to it that our zeal be not meddlesome. There are, how-
ever, some general ways in which we influence, and, if you
please, control this matter of preparatory education. Thus,
the law of supply and demand is not alone applicable to com-
mercial transactions, and is not limited to any particular occu
pations. It enters as an element into all human endeavor; it
governs not quantity of product only, but quality as well. It
controls the quality of the education possessed by the student
when he receives his diploma, just as really as it fixes the
quality of the coat which he wears on the momentous occasion.
Now, every man in taking up any occupation, be it high or low,
hand-work or head-work, does so with the purpose not only of
extracting from it a living, but also of gaining a respectable
position among his associates in the same calling. Ambition
and self-respect prompt to this; but, moreover, repute is a recognized agent in the attainment of material success. The higher
the occupation, the higher, as a rule, becomes this aspiration
for the esteem of one's peers. The proverb, " men, like water,
find their level," embodies a principle upon which every one,
consciously or unconsciously, acts. As a consequence, a pretty
constant relation will always be found between the character
and attainments of the actual members of a profession, and
the character and attainments of those seeking to enter that
profession. For no man will willingly enter an occupation

where he will be received with contempt, and not for long will men crowd into a profession so equipped that they must ever occupy its lowest ranks. And here it is that we who are doctors may powerfully influence those who are to become doctors. Just as by our professional career we set up the standard of demand, so will be the quality of supply. If we, as a body, are thoughtful, intelligent, scientific practitioners, then will the recruits of our ranks be likely to come equipped with scientific and logical habits of mind that will make their practice rational. If we, as a body, are routinists, given to makeshifts, subservient to authority in our arts, then must we look for a larger and larger proportion of beginners who start out with a set of splints to fit all limbs, and a set of prescriptions to suit all stomachs, and who will probably succeed as well as the youth who thought to make a file of his father's old loveletters do duty in a second generation.

Let us now pass to our chief topic of consideration—the Academy as a teacher. How has she taught in the past? How is she teaching now? And in what other ways yet may she be a teacher in the future?

In the past, the Academy has played no mean part as a teacher of the profession in this city. We are apt to accept, as a matter of course, any customary source of profit, intellectual or other, and never to estimate its value. An old teacher of mine used to say, "There are many things which we count little to possess, but which it would be terrible not to have." So, I suppose, only our elder members can rightly appreciate the work of the Academy, as they alone can recall the state of affairs that called for its foundation, and from which it has largely helped the profession to escape. But a fair consideration of the matter will, I think, bring any one to the conclusion that the Academy has been very efficient in the education of the profession in this city, in at least two important ways. These are the first two of the objects set forth in the constitution—namely, the cultivation of the science of medicine, and the elevation of the character and honor of the profession.

The scientific papers that have been presented to this body

during the past thirty years have still a very considerable value.
But a part of them have been embraced in the occasional
volumes of the "Transactions." Any one who wishes to have
an idea of the whole must search the files of many medical
journals. But the worth of these papers to us is no fair cri-
terion of their value to their hearers when first read. Judg-
ing so, we ignore all the effects of time and changed circumstances. If one could be possessed of all the medical knowledge
of to-day, and yet be totally ignorant of its history, he might
lay down Paré's account of the ligature, or Harvey's description
of the circulation of the blood with a contemptuous "every
one knows that." Yes, but every one *did* not know that. Or
to take a less exaggerated example : a well informed student,
reading the works, let us say, of Sir James Simpson, is likely
to remark that the conclusions are much the same as we find in
the best text-books. But you, Mr. President, who called that
great man your friend, could retort, "The text books of to-day
have these conclusions, because Simpson came to them thirty
years ago." The student, who at his ease enjoys all the fruit,
little dreams of the giant force that broke the new ground and
sowed the seed. So, I say, the papers of the Academy, to the
profession of this city, had a value far greater than we, accustomed to all their results, can well imagine.

The second avowed object of the Academy was an ethical
one—"to separate," as it was then tersely put, "the sheep from
the goats"—and this end has never been lost sight of. I know
that the name ethics is often of offensive sound ; that it is sug-
gestive of professional bickerings, and of medical courts-mar-
tial ; and that it does frequently seem that those most familiar
with "the code" have become so by their attempts to evade it.
But it has not been, I conceive, by martinet-like methods that
the Academy has raised the ethical standard, but in quite
another way. Any body of professional men, banded together
for the purpose of mutual help, having as their chief rules fair-
dealing, generous and courteous behavior, by living up to these
rules will be more powerful for good than they could be by
any amount of *espionage* and charge-making. What a mem-

ber fears is not a trial for ethical shortcomings, but the loss
of the esteem of his fellows. He dreads the cold shoulder far
more than any discipline or inflicted penalty. This influence
does not stop with members. If any association really lives
up to its generous rules, it becomes to those beyond its pale
a sort of aristocracy of good behavior, and its example is more
or less distinctly emulated. Of the power that the Academy
has exerted in this way for a generation there can be no
doubt. Let us hope that the tradition will not be lost. We
can afford to be generous with our possessions, but our fellowship we can give only to those who win it by uprightness of
conduct.

The Academy early contemplated the formation of a library,
fully appreciatiⁿg its educational power. It even began the
collection of books in a small way, but while it had no perma-
nent habitation, a working library was practically impossible.
Even the small library that had been formed, for want of lodg-
ing did not remain intact. But with the occupancy of the
present building the library at once became a living thing.
We should not forget how much of the vivifying power came
from the zeal and generosity of the late President. The four
hundred volumes, which were all that could be found at the
opening of the building, grew rapidly through the gifts of
Fellows to be a considerable collection. In three and a half
years it has reached ten thousand volumes, exclusive of pam-
phlets. These are books covering a very wide range of subject and of date; ancient tomes are here, and here are the recent issues of the press. Here is already a rich field for the
searching student, and yet we believe the collection is but in
its infancy. Let me make an appeal to each of you for your
help. This collection of books is made up entirely of gifts.
Some have given profusely of their riches; others have given
less abundantly, but not less earnestly, according to their
means and opportunity. Let no one suppose, as he looks
along his shelves, searching for something he may give to this
library, that anything is too small to offer. The very volume
which to you seems insignificant, may be of great value as

completing a work, or as illustrating something else. No one who has been obliged to undertake any kind of medical research will ever look upon any book as valueless. A common objection is, " I have nothing to give away except a lot of old rubbish—books entirely out of date." Several times in my life I have had " a lot of old rubbish " given to me, but out of it I have picked some of the rarest treasures of my library. Remember that it is nothing to the disparagement of a library that it is rich in old books. While we need not say with Chaucer :

> " For out of the old fieldes, as men saithe
> Cometh all this new corne fro yere to yere,
> And out of old bookes in good faith
> Cometh all this new science that men lere,"

yet we must feel that an old book, if it were ever intrinsically valuable, still is so. It may have the treasures of original research, or the lessons of practical experience. It will have at least that quaint value of showing the same facts, the same questions, the same perplexities that make up our professional life, considered by minds trained in other times, and under other circumstances. For myself, I gratefully acknowledge that more than once, when I had searched fruitlessly through my recent surgical " authorities," I have learned what I wished to know from Astley Cooper or Charles Bell, or even from more ancient men than they. Knowledge is ever increasing and science grows apace, but the calm wisdom of experience is as often to be found in an old book as in a new one.

The Academy has not stopped with the formation of a library. Books are, after all, the conservators of what is known ; the recorders of what is, to a certain extent at least, settled opinion. The daily work of the medical world, its eager searchings, its earnest strivings, find their expression in its periodical literature. In our day of feverish energy and progress, the making of books cannot be waited for. To ask the student of to-day to be content with text-books, would be like asking the Wall Street operator, accustomed to watch the varying record of the telegraphic tape, to be content with the stock report in the secular column of the religious weekly which his honest rustic father reads with edification. The desire for access to the periodicals of the world has found expression among us by the formation of various clubs of greater or less size. The Academy has endeavored to meet this demand by opening its reading-rooms. So greatly have these been appreciated, that it has been obliged to double its accommodations. Henceforward the readers will have at their command one hundred and twenty-five medical journals, bringing the tidings of our profession from every civilized country, and in every European tongue. Every important periodical of Europe and America will be upon our tables. The entire activity of the medical world can be viewed by the student who takes the room above for his point of observation. Mark, moreover, that there is nothing exclusive in all this; the Academy spreads the tables; whosoever will, is at liberty to partake of the feast.

All this the Academy is doing for the reading-class, the studious element of our profession. Let me recall to you the very earnest plea, made with characteristic force and humor, by the distinguished gentleman who gave the address of last year. He urged the claims of another class; of that, namely, which has no time to read —whose every hour is under the dominion of exacting patients. I allude to the subject, not because anything can be added to the earnestness or wit of his statement of the case, but because it is a matter of too great moment to be let drop, or to be long let lie dormant.

It is a need, not only of the overworked practitioner whose woes Dr. Thomson has so graphically depicted – it is a want almost equally felt by those whose special work drives them to special study, but who would, nevertheless, gladly know something of the progress of other branches, and who dread lest their labor in particular fields should seem to deprive them of their birthright in the commonwealth of medicine. The need, then, is evident; moreover, it is a need that has long been foreseen, for among the duties of the Council, as laid down by the Constitution, it is specified "they shall nominate such Fellows as are to be appointed, to deliver series of discourses or lectures on scientific subjects before the Academy." Further, the project seems to have the hearty approval of all those most familiar with the working and resources of the Academy. Able lecturers, certainly, are abundant among our Fellowship. Why is it, then, that this educational agency, confessedly so desirable on all hands, is not put into operation? Apparently, simply because the council cannot ask those whom they would choose as lecturers to give their labor gratuitously, and no fund exists which can be devoted to the purpose. If, then, we are to have the lectures, either some of you distinguished men you whose words, whenever you choose to speak, are listened to with respect and admiration—laying aside your modesty, and recognizing the obligation your eminence imposes upon you, must volunteer; or we must all contribute of our means and appeal to the generous laity, whom we may be able to influence, to form the necessary fund. When we see the lavish liberality of our wealthy men toward institutions of learning, can we believe that if they knew of the opportunity here presented, it would long go unimproved? I feel confident that in one way or another this desideratum is soon to be gained. Let each one of us start out to-night as missionaries in the cause.

This matter of lectureships leads me to another in some measure akin to it. It is now generally recognized that an institution of learning should have at least a double function: That of clearly teaching that which is known, and that of making original investigation into that which is not known. To all the natural sciences our country is making its contributions, as well as being prominent, if not preëminent, in what it is the habit to call " applied science." There is no reason why we should not contribute in like manner to medicine. In the art we are constantly making researches, and if the valuable discoveries in this direction are alone considered, we need not shrink from comparison with any nation since we have had a separate existence. It should be our aim to advance the science as well. But such investigations are generally costly in time and in expenditure. The man immersed in practice cannot give the time ; the young man with the training for the work, and still free to do it, with the enthusiasm that prompts to its undertaking, cannot afford to take from his slender earnings the means for the prosecution of his inquiries. Our inactivity in the more abstract branches of medicine is not because our eyes are less keen, our ears less attentive, our minds less logical, our patience under obstacles less enduring than those of our neighbors. American students in foreign laboratories do as good work as the best. But it is because the daily needs of life leave nothing for science. Research in America is done chiefly in endowed institutions; or, despite some glorious exceptions, by those who contend against the debilitating influences of wealth. Our profession here has the material for a truly scientific class, and the foundation of scholarships would do more to develop this material than any other agency I can think of. And this is another means through which I hope, nay, I confidently expect, that the Academy, in a not distant future, will exert its educational power.

Let me detain you by one more suggestion. Is it not possible for the Academy to found a Museum? I shall not waste your time in discussing the value of museums, as this is quite fully recognized. " But why another? " some may ask. Are there not enough, and good ones in the city? If museums are good, there can hardly be too many. We have indeed several good museums : some, like that of the New York Hospital, containing the trophies of a long career ; others, like the Wood Museum, monuments to great personal energy and industry. But the museum the Academy might found would in no way, I conceive, conflict with, or divert from such museums as these. The existence of the great museum of the Royal College of Surgeons has not prevented the growth of the collections of the great hospitals of London. The museums of hospitals and of colleges will always, I presume, be increased by the contributions of those connected directly or by affiliation with those institutions. The great mass of the profession remains unappealed to. If they preserve specimens, they are hidden in their closets. They do not care to part with them

2

to collections in which they have no personal interest. Much valuable material is thus lost to the student, and generally lost entirely. If the Academy had a museum, I believe that very much would be saved. You have seen how liberally the profession has given its books during the past three years. Were there no libraries in New York before, to which these might have been given? Certainly there were. Were there no books to spare before? Certainly, again. The Academy appealed to givers in a way they could not resist, because they were interested in answering the appeal. So it doubtless would be of all that can illustrate the art and science of medicine, if the Academy should undertake to be its custodian. It is probable, moreover, that many a practitioner who is now indifferent, would collect specimens if he found his trouble could be made subservient to a general good. The hospital and college museums would grow as before, and from the same sources as now, and from the stimulus of rivalry with still greater rapidity, while the Academy museum would garner the harvest from quite fresh fields.

I am but too well aware that I have presented for your consideration nothing new; I can scarcely flatter myself that I have presented old thoughts in a new light. I have endeavored simply to trace the career of the Academy as a Teacher: in the past by the production of scientific papers and by elevating the standard of professional character; in the present by the additional power of its Library and its Reading-room. I have also pointed out some directions in which its educational force might be still farther exerted. These projects are not Utopian; they are all feasible, if further consideration shall prove them advisable; indeed, the germ of them all already exists. If, by this rehearsal, I have brought back to you the consciousness that, as Fellows of this Academy, you are " citizens of no mean city; " and if, especially, I have stimulated you to stay up the hands of those who are so wisely and zealously leading us, my aim has been fully accomplished. How can we fail to have high hopes of the Academy? Its situation is peculiarly fortunate. It is hampered in its work by no official restrictions. It is not an association devoted to special studies, nor to narrow special ends. Its aims are broad and catholic—all that may advance our common art. It is controlled by no clique; it is the mouthpiece of no faction; it is rather the common meeting-ground of the best elements of our professional body. To the material advantages of a definite habitation, of growing resources, of a large yet selected membership, it adds the power of age, of character, of authority. If, with all this, the Academy fails to be in the future a great power for professional good, it will be because in some way or other we are delinquent. Let us see to it, then, each and every one of us, that our professional lives be her fair "epistles known and read of all men;" let us strive to liken her halls to " the groves of the Academy where Plato taught the truth."